The Gold Ring

The focus in this book is on the graphemes

o, oa, ow, o-e

going gold rolled almost

toad

followed

mole hole nose throne home

One day Bean was going along the path to the pond when a gold ring rolled past him.

The gold ring rolled to the edge of

the grass and it disappeared. Bean

went to look for it.

Suddenly a mole popped his head out of a hole next to the grass. The gold ring was hanging from his nose.

The mole was almost blind. He
could not see Bean. He climbed out
of the hole and the ring fell off his
nose.

Bean was looking for the ring when a toad suddenly jumped out of the grass. The ring was round one of its legs.

Bean wanted the ring. He followed

the toad to a pool of muddy water.

He could not see the gold ring.

Just when Bean thought the ring

was lost the toad hopped out of the

pool. The ring was still round its leg.

Bean followed the toad as it
hopped through the grass by the
side of the path, but he could not
catch it.

Then the toad jumped into the pond.

It swam under the water until it

came up on a lily leaf.

The toad looked like a king on a

throne with a crown on its head.

Bean would never get the ring now.

He gave up and he went home.

Vowel graphemes

ay/a-e:	day came gave
ee/ea:	see leaf Bean
i/y/i-e/:	blind climbed by side like
oa/ow/o-e/o:	toad followed nose throne home mole hole gold almost rolled going
oo:	pool
oo:	look looking looked
ow/ou:	crown now out round
or:	for
ear:	disappeared
er:	under water never
ea:	head